The Orchestra

Richard Spilsbury

Raintree is an imprint of Capstone Global Library Limited, a company incorporated in England and Wales having its registered office at 264 Banbury Road, Oxford, OX2 7DY – Registered company number: 6695582

www.raintree.co.uk
myorders@raintree.co.uk

Edited by Clare Lewis
Designed by Terri Poburka
Original illustrations © Capstone Global Library Limited 2018
Picture research by Svetlana Zhurkin
Production by Kathy McColley
Originated by Capstone Global Library Ltd
Printed and bound in India

ISBN 978 1 4747 4931 2   ISBN 978 1 4747 4932 9
22 21 20 19 18   23 22 21 20 19
10 9 8 7 6 5 4 3 2 1   10 9 8 7 6 5 4 3 2 1

British Library Cataloguing in Publication Data
A full catalogue record for this book is available from the British Library.

Acknowledgements
We would like to thank the following for permission to reproduce photographs: Alamy: Lebrecht Music and Arts Photo Library, 21 (middle and bottom), Music-Images, 29 (top right); Dreamstime: Ihb, 27 (top), Jackq, 16 (bottom left); Getty Images: Corbis/George Rinhart, 29 (middle left), Dorling Kindersley, 16 (top right), 23 (top right), 25 (middle), Hiroyuki Ito, 26 (top), Hulton Archive, 29 (middle right); iStockphoto: 2windspa, 25 (top), FierceAbin, 28 (bottom right), nano, 13 (bottom), Photo_Concepts, 17 (top); Newscom: Album/Fine Art Images, 29 (top left), SIPA/ISIFA/Michale Hradecky, 27 (bottom), SIPA/Sebastien Salom-Gomis, 26 (bottom), The Times/David Bebber, 29 (bottom right), WENN/Graeme Richardson, 27 (middle left and right), Zuma Press/Panoramic, 29 (bottom left); Shutterstock: A_Lesik, 4 (bottom), 5 (top left and right), 8 (bottom), Africa Studio, 5 (bottom), 9 (middle left), Alenavlad, 16 (top left), Andrey_Popov, 16 (bottom right), Baishev, 22 (bottom left), ben smith, 15 (right), Boris Medvedev, 22 (top and middle), Cabeca de Marmore, 23 (top left), Chatchawat Prasertsom, 4 (top), Chromakey, 19 (bottom), Claudio Divizia, cover (musical notes), Dmitry Skutin, 20 (right), Dmitry Vereshchagin, 11 (bottom right), 20 (left), Elena Schweitzer, 22 (bottom right), elenabsl, 6-7, Everett Historical, 28 (top left and right, bottom left), evgeniyjm, 15 (left), 17 (bottom left), furtseff, cover (top and bottom), 21 (top right), Horatiu Bota, 18 (bottom), klerik78, 11 (bottom left), Martin Good, 8 (top and top middle), 9 (bottom), Matthias G. Ziegler, 17 (bottom right), Mehmet Cetin, 12–13, Miguel Garcia Saavedra, 14 (left), 18 (middle), Mike Flippo, 21 (top left), Milkovasa, 11 (top right), mkm3, 15 (middle), mulder32, 10 (right), Pavel K, back cover, posztos, 9 (middle right), sbarabu, 24, Sergei Butorin, 8 (bottom middle), Stokkete, cover (middle), 4 (middle), 14 (right), 18 (top), Sutthimon Ounnapiruk, 10 (left), Teerawit Chankowet, 11 (top left), the palms, 19 (top), Tommy Kay, 23 (bottom), Tropical studio, 26 (middle), wacpan, 9 (top), Zheltyshev, 25 (bottom)

Design Elements by Shutterstock

Contents

Some words are shown in bold, **like this**. You can find out what they mean by looking in the glossary.

Get to know orchestras

Orchestras are groups of **musicians** playing musical instruments together. They usually play **classical** music on many different instruments. The instruments are divided into four main families depending on how they make sounds.

Strings

Woodwinds

Strings These wooden instruments usually have four strings. Musicians move a **bow** over the strings to make a sound. Sometimes musicians **pluck** the strings with their fingers too.

Woodwinds These tube-shaped instruments have many holes along them. Musicians blow air into them to make sounds. Some are made from wood, but others are metal or plastic.

Brass Brass instruments are metal and tube-shaped. They are often made from a gold-coloured metal called brass. Brass instruments make loud sounds when players blow air into them.

Brass

Percussion

Keyboards

Percussion These include instruments such as drums, bells and tambourines. Musicians hit, shake or scrape them to make a wide range of sounds.

Keyboards Keyboards are not a family on their own. they are part of the percussion family. Keyboards have a set of bars called keys. Musicians press the **keys** down to make sounds.

Classical music
This style of music is most often played by orchestras. It is written down to show the notes the different instruments need to play. The oldest classical pieces are from the 17th century and the newest from the 21st century.

Stave
The stave is the five lines that the notes are written on.

Note
Notes are symbols showing how high, low and long a sound needs to be.

The orchestra in action

In an orchestra, the **musicians** playing each family of instruments usually sit or stand together in different sections.

Percussion section
The percussion instruments are across the back of the orchestra. A few musicians may play several different percussion instruments during a **concert**.

Keyboard section
There is usually one keyboard instrument in an orchestra, such as a piano or organ.

String section
There are more string instruments in the orchestra than all the other instruments put together. This is because they make a quiet sound.

Principal violinist
The principal violinist is the orchestra leader.

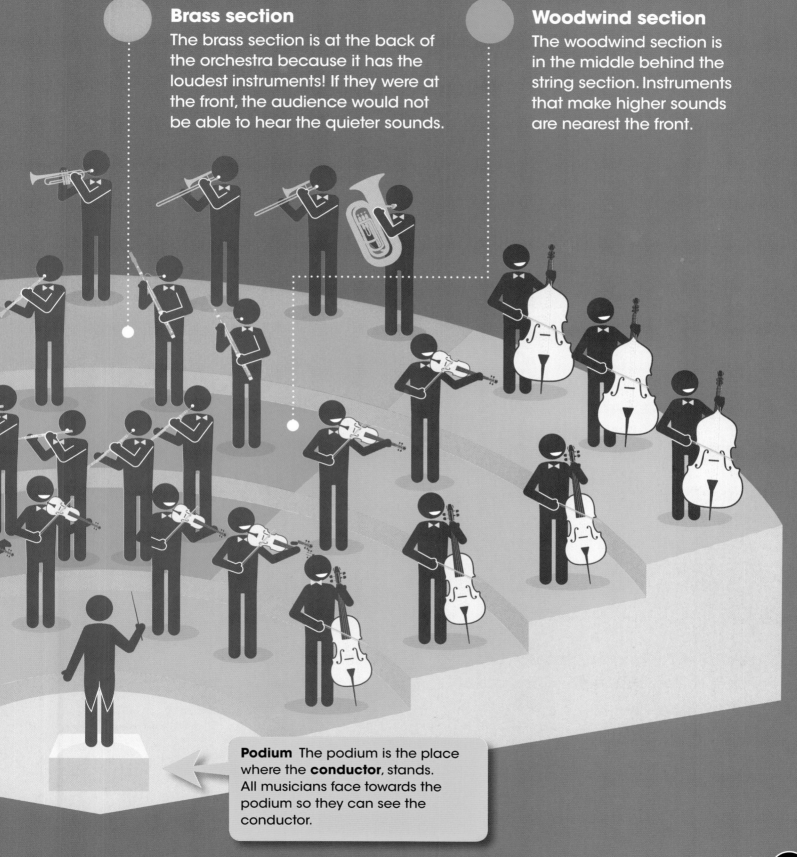

Brass section

The brass section is at the back of the orchestra because it has the loudest instruments! If they were at the front, the audience would not be able to hear the quieter sounds.

Woodwind section

The woodwind section is in the middle behind the string section. Instruments that make higher sounds are nearest the front.

Podium The podium is the place where the **conductor**, stands. All musicians face towards the podium so they can see the conductor.

Performances

The musicians who make up an orchestra train for many years to play their instrument well. They practise together for many hours to make sure they play perfectly for a performance in a concert hall.

Conductor This is the person who leads and controls the orchestra's performance. Conductors make sure the musicians play at the right speed, play loud or soft, and start and finish together.

Soloist This is a musician who plays alone for part of a performance, usually with backing music from the orchestra. A soloist often sits or stands at the front of the stage.

First violinists These violin players usually carry the main tune. The leader of the first violins often does short violin solos.

Rehearsal A **rehearsal** is a session when performers practise the music they will play for a performance together.

Conductor

Soloist

First violins

Rehearsal

Score This is a copy of the music the orchestra plays. A score shows all the notes to be played by every instrument in the orchestra.

Choir A choir is a group of singers who take part in performances of some orchestral pieces.

Baton The conductor moves this stick through the air to tell musicians what to do.

Score

Choir

Baton

Concert hall
This is the building where an orchestra performs.

Audience
The audience is the group of people who come to watch and listen to an orchestra.

Concert
A concert is a musical performance given by an orchestra. Concerts can last for hours!

String instruments

The string instrument family contains four instruments that look similar in shape but are very different sizes. The smallest one, the violin, has shorter thinner strings than the largest one, the double bass. That is why the violin plays higher notes than the double bass.

Violin The violin plays the highest notes of all the members of the string family. It is held between the chin and left shoulder. Violin strings are arranged from high to low.

Violin

Cello

Double bass

Viola A viola is slightly larger than a violin. It has thicker strings. It is played in the same way as a violin but makes a deeper, richer sound.

Cello A cello is bigger than a viola. Its bigger body and longer strings produce deeper sounds than the viola. Players sit down to play the cello and hold the instrument upright.

Double bass This is the largest string instrument. Its long strings make the lowest sounds of all the stringed instruments. Players stand or sit on a stool with the double bass upright.

Harp A harp has a big, triangle-shaped wooden frame. It has about 45 strings stretched from top to bottom. The strings vary in length and thickness, so they play different notes when plucked.

Harp

double bass   cello   viola   violin

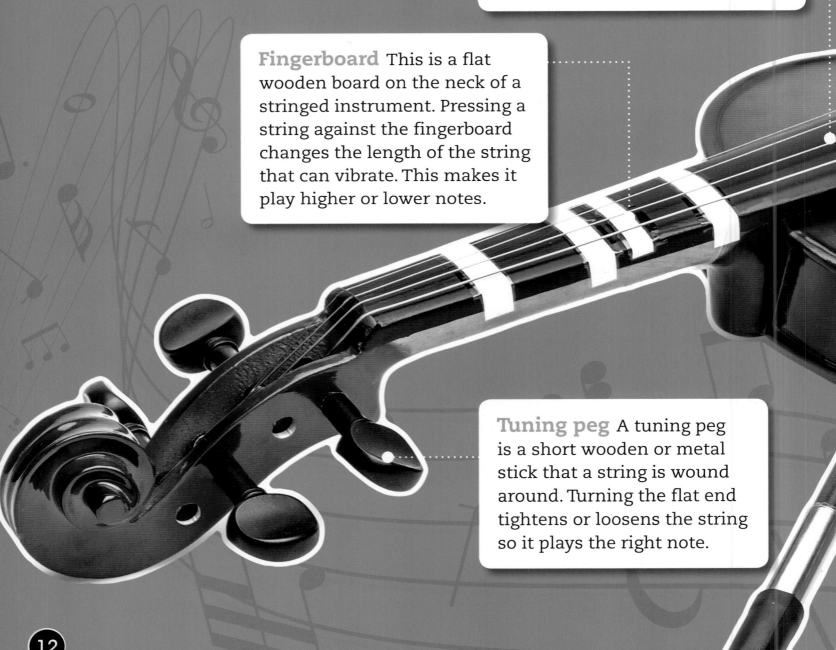

String instruments make sounds when their strings **vibrate**, or move to and fro. Musicians change notes by pressing their fingers up and down the fingerboard. At the same time, they move their bows across the strings.

Strings Strings are long thin pieces of nylon or metal. Sometimes they are made of animal guts. Long, thick, heavy or looser strings vibrate slower and make lower sounds than shorter, thinner, lighter or tighter strings.

Fingerboard This is a flat wooden board on the neck of a stringed instrument. Pressing a string against the fingerboard changes the length of the string that can vibrate. This makes it play higher or lower notes.

Tuning peg A tuning peg is a short wooden or metal stick that a string is wound around. Turning the flat end tightens or loosens the string so it plays the right note.

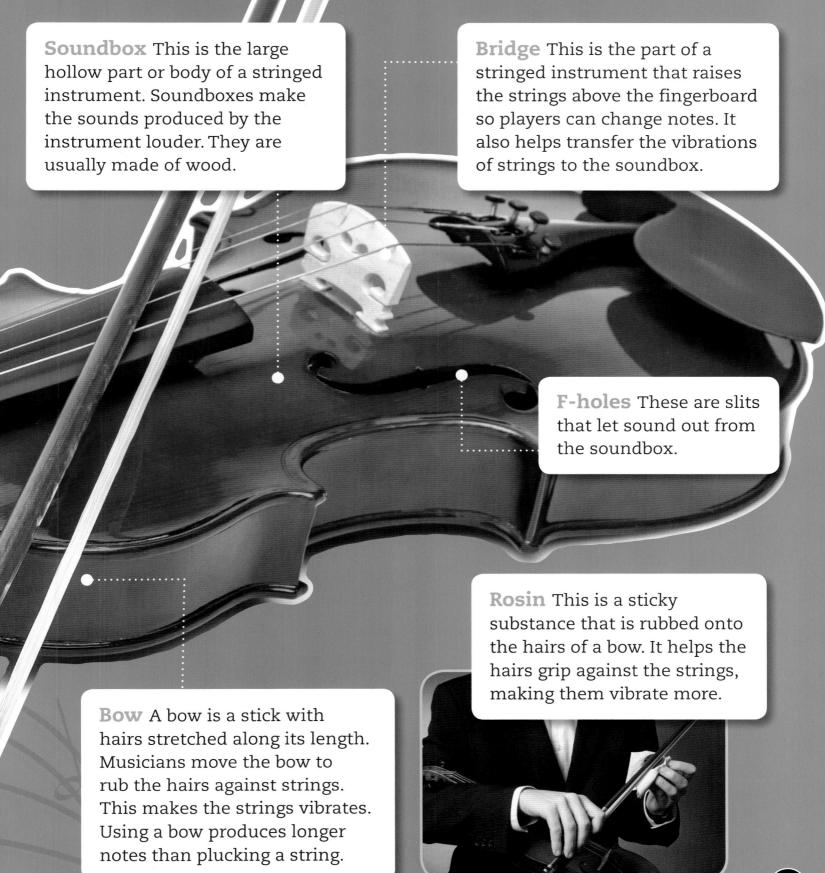

Soundbox This is the large hollow part or body of a stringed instrument. Soundboxes make the sounds produced by the instrument louder. They are usually made of wood.

Bridge This is the part of a stringed instrument that raises the strings above the fingerboard so players can change notes. It also helps transfer the vibrations of strings to the soundbox.

F-holes These are slits that let sound out from the soundbox.

Rosin This is a sticky substance that is rubbed onto the hairs of a bow. It helps the hairs grip against the strings, making them vibrate more.

Bow A bow is a stick with hairs stretched along its length. Musicians move the bow to rub the hairs against strings. This makes the strings vibrates. Using a bow produces longer notes than plucking a string.

Woodwind instruments

When a musician blows air through a woodwind instrument, it makes the air inside vibrate. Sounds come out of the hole at the end. There are also holes along the instrument. The musician changes the notes by covering or uncovering these holes with his or her fingers. This changes the length that the air travels when vibrating. Blowing harder makes air vibrate more, making louder sounds.

Flute This is a woodwind instrument held sideways with both hands. A musician plays it by blowing across a hole in the mouthpiece on top.

Flute

Recorder A recorder is a simple instrument. It is shaped like a tube and has eight holes. The musician blows into it and changes notes by covering the holes with his or her fingers.

Recorder

Bass flute

Piccolo

Piccolo A piccolo is a shorter version of the flute. Piccolos play the highest, most piercing notes of all the woodwind instruments.

Bass flute This is a long flute that plays lower notes than the flute. It is curled over at the top so players can reach keys along its length.

Reeds or no reeds?

Reeds are thin strips of wood or plastic attached to the mouthpiece. Blowing into the mouthpiece and over the reed makes it vibrate quickly. This starts vibrations of the air inside the instrument. Recorders and flutes have no reeds, but clarinets, saxophones, oboes and bassoons and some other woodwind instruments do.

Oboe An oboe is a straight wooden woodwind instrument. It has two thin reeds sticking out of the mouthpiece that vibrate together. Musicians hold it like a recorder. Oboes make slightly lower sounds than flutes.

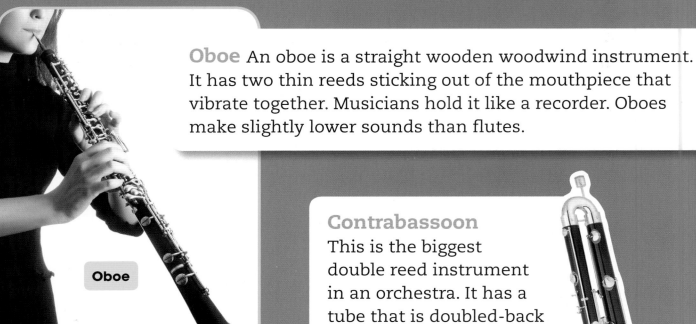

Oboe

Contrabassoon

This is the biggest double reed instrument in an orchestra. It has a tube that is doubled-back twice. This allows the player to change notes along its length. The contrabassoon plays some of the lowest notes in the orchestra.

Contrabassoon

Clarinet

A clarinet is a long, straight wooden instrument. Its single reed is held onto the mouthpiece using a strap called a ligature. It is played like an oboe with the bell pointing outwards.

Cor Anglais A Cor Anglais is longer and wider than an oboe and it makes lower sounds. It has a double reed: two reeds that vibrate against each other when a musician blows against them.

Cor Anglais

Mouthpiece

Clarinet

Bassoon A bassoon is a very long, doubled-back woodwind instrument. It is held upright with its bell pointing upwards. Players blow into a double reed at the end of a curved metal tube.

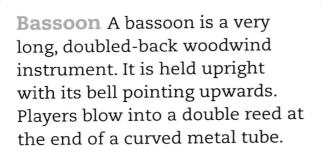

Bassoon

Bass clarinet

This is the biggest type of clarinet. It is so long that its top and bottom are bent so musicians can play it. The bass clarinet plays some of the lowest notes in the orchestra.

Bass clarinet

Alto saxophone

This woodwind instrument is usually made of brass and it has a single reed. Alto saxophones have a bent neck and upturned bell. They play high, bright sounding notes.

Alto saxophone

Brass instruments

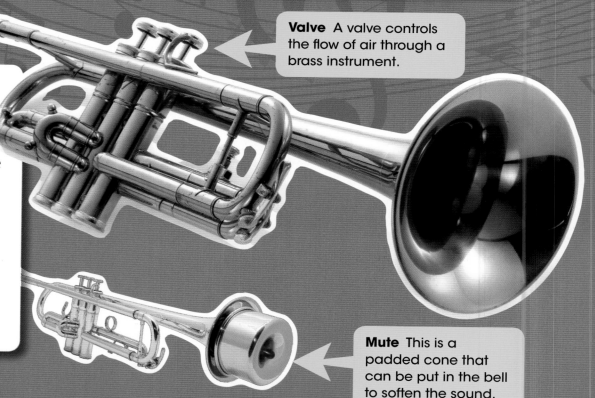

This family of instruments can play louder than any other in the orchestra. Brass players blow raspberries into the mouthpiece with their lips! This makes the air inside brass instruments start to vibrate to make sounds. Players change notes on brass instruments usually by pressing on three valves that shorten or lengthen the amount of air vibrating inside.

French horn This brass instrument has a tube coiled into a circle that gets gradually wider towards its large bell. It is played with the bell curving downwards. The French horn produces the widest range of notes on a brass instrument.

Valve A valve controls the flow of air through a brass instrument.

Trumpet
This is one of the smallest brass instruments. Its tube is curved and bent into long loops and it has a wide bell. Trumpets are held horizontally to play and they make a high, bright sound.

Mute This is a padded cone that can be put in the bell to soften the sound.

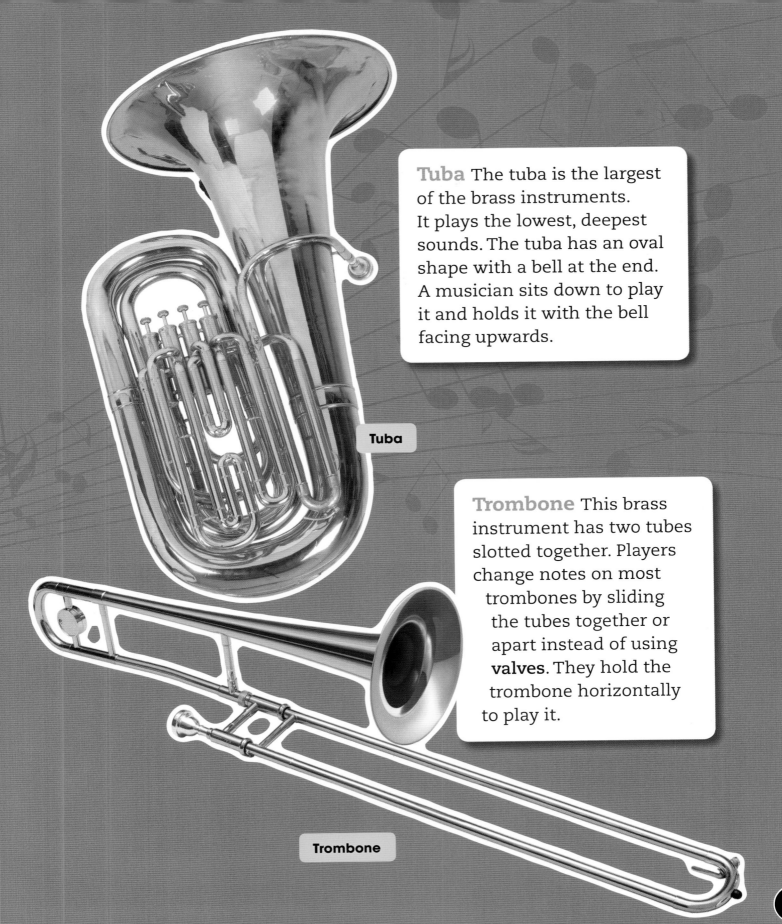

Tuba The tuba is the largest of the brass instruments. It plays the lowest, deepest sounds. The tuba has an oval shape with a bell at the end. A musician sits down to play it and holds it with the bell facing upwards.

Tuba

Trombone This brass instrument has two tubes slotted together. Players change notes on most trombones by sliding the tubes together or apart instead of using **valves**. They hold the trombone horizontally to play it.

Trombone

Percussion instruments

Percussion instruments also make a wide variety of sounds that add to the music's mood. Percussionists hit their instruments with hard sticks or soft-ended **mallets** to make them vibrate and produce harsh or soft sounds. Keyboards are also percussion instruments.

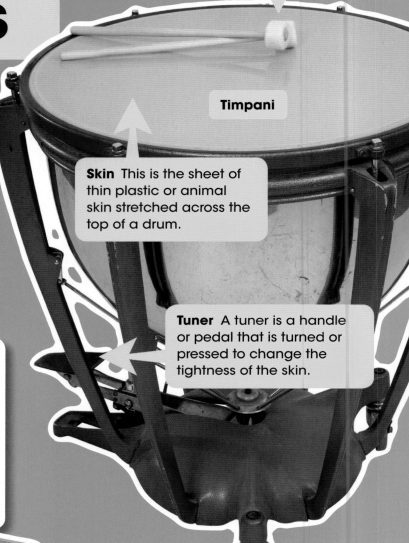

Mallets

Timpani

Skin This is the sheet of thin plastic or animal skin stretched across the top of a drum.

Tuner A tuner is a handle or pedal that is turned or pressed to change the tightness of the skin.

Xylophone This instrument has wooden bars a musician can hit with a mallet.. Each wooden bar has a different length so it makes a different note. Metal tubes attached below the bars trap air that vibrates to make the xylophone notes louder and longer.

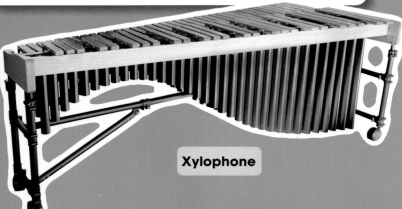

Xylophone

Timpani Timpani are large bowl-shaped drums with metal bodies. Players hit the drum skins with mallets or sticks to make them vibrate. Each drum is **tuned** to a different note by making the skin looser or tighter.

Marimba

Vibraphone

Marimba A marimba is a larger version of a xylophone. It has longer bars that make a full, mellow sound.

Vibraphone This instrument is like a xylophone but it has metal bars and metal tubes. They have electric spinning discs inside. These discs help the vibraphone play long, trembling notes.

Glockenspiel

Glockenspiel The glockenspiel is a miniature xylophone. It has metal bars that are struck using sticks tipped with wooden balls. There are no tubes below the bars. The glockenspiel makes sounds like tinkling bells.

Tubular bells These are metal tubes of different lengths hung from a metal frame. Each tube plays a different note. The tubes are hit with a mallet and they sound like bells ringing in a church.

Tubular bells

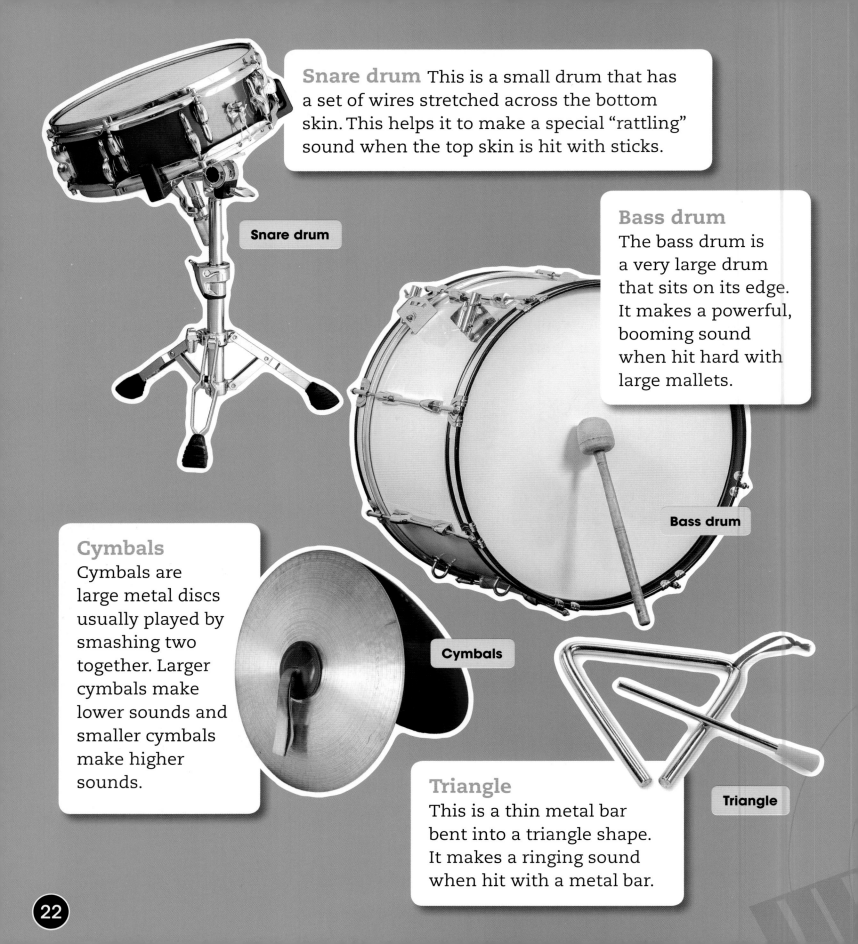

Snare drum This is a small drum that has a set of wires stretched across the bottom skin. This helps it to make a special "rattling" sound when the top skin is hit with sticks.

Snare drum

Bass drum
The bass drum is a very large drum that sits on its edge. It makes a powerful, booming sound when hit hard with large mallets.

Bass drum

Cymbals
Cymbals are large metal discs usually played by smashing two together. Larger cymbals make lower sounds and smaller cymbals make higher sounds.

Cymbals

Triangle
This is a thin metal bar bent into a triangle shape. It makes a ringing sound when hit with a metal bar.

Triangle

Castanets

Castanets Castanets are two pieces of wood tied together. They make a clickety-clack sound when hit against each other.

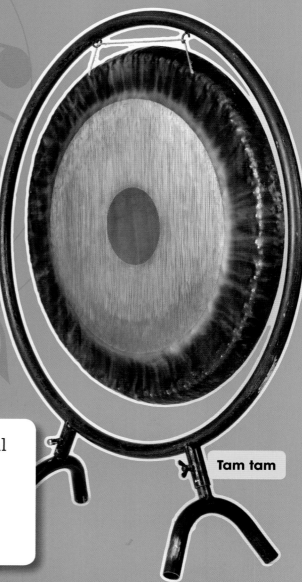

Tam tam

Tam tam A tam tam is a very large metal plate with a raised centre. It hangs from a metal pipe. Tam tams make sounds when hit in the centre with a mallet. The sound gets louder after it is hit!

Tuned or untuned?

Tuned percussion instruments like the xylophone and timpani have different length bars or a skin that can be made tighter or looser. This means they can make different notes. **Untuned** percussion instruments, like the triangle or wood block, play just one note.

Wood block — This is a hollow block of hard wood that make cracking or knocking sounds when struck with a wooden stick.

Keyboard instruments

Keyboard instruments are part of the percussion section. People play keyboard instruments by pressing keys with their fingers. Different keys play different notes and musicians can play many notes at the same time. Many keyboards have pedals that can make notes louder, softer, longer, or play other notes. Some keyboards have knobs, buttons and levers to change the type of sound too.

Piano The piano is a keyboard instrument with 88 keys. Pressing keys makes soft hammers hit strings of different lengths inside. Releasing keys stops the strings from vibrating, unless a pedal is pushed to make the sound longer.

Piano

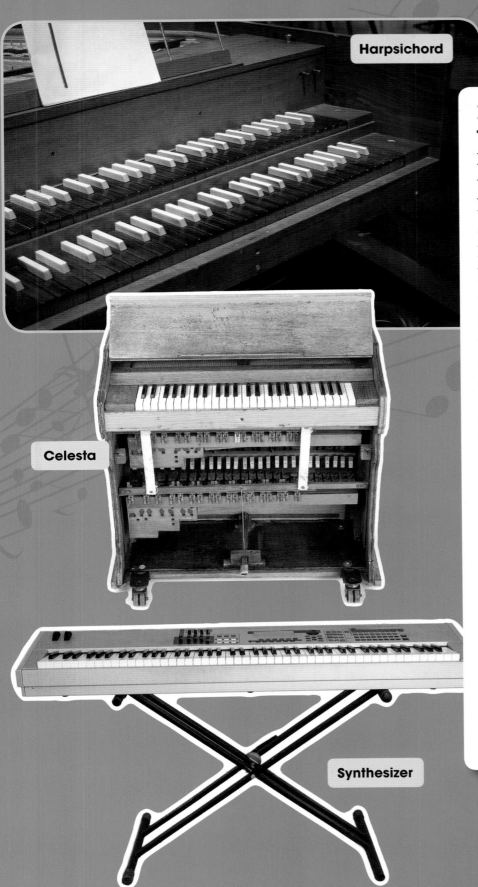

Harpsichord

Harpsichord

This is an early type of piano. Harpsichords often have two keyboards. Pressing a key on a harpsichord makes a small pick pluck a string. Harpsichords cannot play louder or softer notes.

Celesta

The celesta resembles a small upright piano. Pressing a key hits a mallet inside against a metal bar, rather like those in a glockenspiel. The celesta makes delicate, bell-like sounds.

Celesta

Synthesizer

This is an electronic keyboard instrument. Pressing the keys makes electricity flow in patterns that can be converted into many different sounds. Synthesizers can sound like other instruments, natural sounds or even sound like nothing else!

Synthesizer

Different orchestras

Around the world there are different types of orchestras, which often use distinct kinds of instruments. Some play **traditional** music that is not the classical style typical of Europe or the United States.

Gagaku This is the oldest orchestra in Japan. It includes 16 to 30 instruments such as drums, a mouth organ, flutes, gong and strings. The first Gagaku orchestra performed only for Japan's royal family.

Gamelan Gamelan orchestras are from Indonesia. They are made up mainly of tuned percussion instruments such as gongs, drums and xylophones, but there are often flutes and stringed instruments too.

Andalusian orchestra This orchestra has singers, stringed instruments, oboes and more unusual instruments. Andalusian orchestras play music that once came from southern Spain with words written by Muslims and Jews in Arabic and Hebrew.

Mariachi This type of orchestra is from Mexico. Modern mariachi use a variety of different guitars, as well as violins and trumpets. Mariachi musicians often dress as Mexican cowboys!

Ice orchestra This unusual orchestra from Sweden has instruments carved from ice! It plays in an igloo-shaped ice concert hall in winter. The instruments make a clear, haunting sound.

Ukulele orchestra These orchestras are completely made up of ukuleles! They play fun, foot-tapping versions of familiar tunes.

Famous composers

There are many great composers who wrote music for orchestras. New music is written for orchestras every day!

Johann Sebastian Bach

Born: 1685; *Died:* 1750

From: Germany

Famous Music: The Brandenburg Concertos; Mass in B Minor

Quick Fact: He became an orphan at the age of ten so his oldest brother had to look after him.

Wolfgang Amadeus Mozart

Born: 1756; *Died:* 1791

From: Austria

Famous Music: Operas like *The Magic Flute; Symphony No. 40 in G minor; Eine Kleine Nachtmusik*

Quick Fact: This child genius could play violin and harpsichord better than most adults!

Ludwig van Beethoven

Born: 1770; *Died:* 1827

From: Germany

Famous Music: Fifth and Ninth Symphonies; Moonlight Sonata

Quick Fact: He wrote his most powerful and dramatic music after he became deaf aged 30.

Pyotr Ilyich Tchaikovsky

Born: 1840; *Died:* 1893

From: Russia

Famous Music: Romeo and Juliet; the 1812 Overture; the ballets *The Nutcracker, Swan Lake,* and *The Sleeping Beauty*

Quick Fact: Mystery surrounds the real cause of his death in 1893.

Claude Debussy

Born: 1862; **Died:** 1918

From: France

Famous Music: *Clair de Lune; Prelude to the Afternoon of a Faun;* the opera *The Sea*

Quick Fact: At one time, he was so poor he exchanged a composition for coal to light his fire. He called it *Evenings Lighted by Burning Coals.*

Heitor Villa Lobos

Born: 1887; **Died:** 1959

From: Brazil

Famous Music: *Choros; Bachianas Brasileiras*

Quick Fact: He loved Bach and *Bachianas Brasileiras* means Brazilian music in the style of Bach!

Sergei Prokofiev

Born: 1891; **Died:** 1953

From: Russia

Famous Music: *Peter and the Wolf;* the ballet *Romeo and Juliet;* the *Second Violin Concerto*

Quick Fact: He began writing music at the age of five.

Aaron Copland

Born: 1900; **Died:** 1990

From: America

Famous Music: *Fanfare for Common Man; Rodeo; Appalachian Spring*

Quick Fact: He wrote music that used folk songs and jazz to create a new style.

Max Richter

Born: 1966

From: Germany

Famous Music: *Sleep; Three Worlds: Music from Woolf Works*

Quick Fact: He described his composition *Sleep* as an 8-hour long lullaby.

Hannah Kendall

Born: 1984

From: Britain

Famous Music: *Double Concerto; Aviary Sketches*

Quick Fact: She wrote a piece for 100 violas that was performed at Edinburgh zoo!

Glossary

bow stick with hairs stretched along its length. Musicians move the bow to rub the hairs against strings.

classical traditional style of music most often played by orchestras

composition piece of music that has been written down

concert musical performance with an audience

conductor person who leads and controls the orchestra's performance

key lever that is pressed down on a keyboard to make a sound

mallet wooden hammer

mouthpiece part of a woodwind or brass instrument into which the musician blows

musician someone who plays a musical instrument

pluck to sound a string instrument with your finger, rather than a bow

rehearsal when people practise together before a real performance

traditional music that has been played for a long time. Different countries have different styles of traditional music.

tuned instruments that can play many notes are tuned

ukulele small four-stringed guitar, originally from Hawaii

untuned instruments that can only play one note are untuned

valve part of a brass instrument that opens and shuts to let air through or to stop air

vibrate to move very quickly to and fro. When strings or air move very quickly, they make sounds.

Find out more

Books

Read this book to learn more about the different instruments, what they look and sound like, and how they belong in different families:
My First Orchestra Book, Genevieve Helsby (Naxos Books, 2014)

This book retells Tchaikovsky's Nutcracker ballet story and it has buttons you can press to hear the music.
The Nutcracker: Press the Note to Hear Tchaikovsky's Music (The Story Orchestra) Jessica Courtney-Tickle (Frances Lincoln Children's Books, 2017)

This book has buttons to press so you can hear the sounds of different instruments as you follow the story:
Poppy and the Orchestra: With 16 musical instrument sounds!, Magali Le Huche (Walter Foster Jr, 2017)

This book will help you to learn about classical music, the theory behind music, and the fun you can have making it.
The School of Music, Meurig Bowen & Rachel Bowen (Wide Eyed Editions, 2017)

Music to listen to

The Young Person's Guide To The Orchestra by Benjamin Britten
This takes you on an epic tour of the instruments of the orchestra, with some very catchy music.

Peter and the Wolf by Sergei Prokofiev
In this piece of music a storyteller reads a children's story while the orchestra illustrates it. Each character has a leitmotif: a sound that we hear every time they appear. It makes a great introduction to the instruments of the orchestra.

The Nutcracker Suite by Pyotr Ilyich Tchaikovsky
The music behind the story set on Christmas Eve when toys come to life has character, colour and often instantly recognisable tunes.

Carnival of the Animals by Camille Saint-Saens
Different animals are represented at different times in this piece of music. See if you can guess which are which!

Piano Sonata in D major K.448 – First movement by Wolfgang Amadeus Mozart
It is said that students who listen to this for ten minutes before taking a test get better scores!

Websites

On this website you can explore different instruments of the orchestra and hear them being played: **www.philharmonia.co.uk/explore/instruments**

To learn more about how the instruments of the orchestra make their sounds, go to: **www.arapahoe-phil.org/learn/resources-instruments-orchestra/**

On this website you can click on links to find interviews with musicians and demonstrations of orchestral instruments: **www.khanacademy.org/humanities/music/music-instruments-orchestra**

Index